Prais

OCTOBER MOURNING

A Song

A STON

AN AMERIC

BEST FICTION F

★ "Beautifully realized. . . . Both intellectually and aesthetically engaging."
—*Booklist* (starred review)

"From those of us who suffered through the terrible maelstrom
surrounding Matt's murder to those of you who worried, who
wondered, who imagined, what it was like, this touching work
is a somber gift to you."
—Jason Marsden, executive vice president, the Matthew Shepard Foundation

"The poems in Newman's *October Mourning* build over the course of
the verse novel, creatively bringing sundry elements of the event into
an anthropomorphic light, the tragedy of Mr. Shepard's death slowly
growing until the reader is left with a profound sense of loss, perhaps
even tears." —*Lambda Literary*

"A brilliant example of various poetic forms. . . . This book is
incredibly thought-provoking and will have a gut-wrenching impact."
—*Library Media Connection*

"Treats a difficult subject with sensitivity and directness. . . . These
poems are sure to instill much-needed empathy and awareness to
gay issues in today's teens." —*Kirkus Reviews*

"What impact will the depiction of such an event have on today's
teens? Put simply—a tremendous impact. Newman's verse is both
masterful and steady-handed. Each poem is beautiful in its subtle
sophistication. . . . Many teens will see how far we've come, while
others will see how far we still have to go." —*School Library Journal*

OCTOBER MOURNING

A Song for Matthew Shepard

Lesléa Newman

CANDLEWICK PRESS

October Mourning: A Song for Matthew Shepard
is a work of poetic imagination.

Copyright © 2012 by Lesléa Newman

Photograph on page v used courtesy of the Matthew Shepard Foundation

Photograph on page 117 copyright © by Plynn Gutman

First paperback edition 2020

The Library of Congress has cataloged the hardcover edition as follows:

Newman, Lesléa.
October mourning : a song for Matthew Shepard / Lesléa Newman. — 1st ed.
p.   cm.
Summary: Relates, from various points of view, events from the night of
October 6, 1998, when twenty-one-year-old Matthew Shepard, a gay college student,
was lured out of a Wyoming bar, savagely beaten, tied to a fence, and left to die.
Includes bibliographical references.
ISBN 978-0-7636-5807-6 (hardcover)
1. Shepard, Matthew, d. 1998 — Juvenile fiction. 2. Laramie (Wyo.) — Fiction.
[1. Novels in verse. 2. Shepard, Matthew, d. 1998 — Fiction. 3. Murder — Fiction.
4. Gays — Fiction. 5. Hate crimes — Fiction.] I. Title.
PZ7.5.N49Oct 2012
[Fic] — dc23   2011048358

ISBN 978-1-5362-1577-9 (paperback)

20 21 22 23 24 25 TRC 10 9 8 7 6 5 4 3 2 1

Printed in Eagan, MN, USA

This book was typeset in Stone Print.

Candlewick Press
99 Dover Street
Somerville, Massachusetts 02144

www.candlewick.com

For Matthew Wayne Shepard
December 1, 1976–October 12, 1998

You are the light of the world.
—*Matthew 5:14–16*

Foreword

I am Matthew's mom. His friends knew him by a variety of other nicknames. But he was always Matt to us.

When Matt was twenty-one and a college student at the University of Wyoming, two local men about his age spotted him in a downtown tavern and perceived him to be gay and therefore vulnerable. They also assumed that he had money because he was wearing clean clothes. According to their statements, they decided to pretend to be gay to befriend him with the ultimate goal of robbing him. He left the tavern with them and, according to their statements, once they were in their vehicle, they said, "We're not gay and you're going to get jacked." They demanded his wallet, which he handed over immediately. But they continued to hit him while driving and eventually ended up outside Laramie, on a dirt road ending at a buck fence. They pulled Matt out of the pickup, tied him to the bottom rail of the fence, and continued to hit him with the butt of a .357 Magnum pistol, swinging it like a bat. They took his shoes and drove off, leaving him tied to the fence.

Back in Laramie, they told their girlfriends they thought they had "just killed a faggot." They then proceeded to destroy evidence. Eighteen hours later, a mountain biker found Matt and called for help. Matt was transported to the Laramie hospital, but his injuries were beyond their care, so he was transported to Fort Collins. During the eighteen hours that Matt was alone on the prairie, his attackers were involved in another incident, and this led law enforcement to put all the pieces together and arrest the two men as well as their girlfriends.

The girlfriends turned state's evidence and were given probation. The two men were sentenced to two consecutive life sentences. As a family, we will never have to deal with them again.

I have resisted exploring anything that relates to Matt's murder. It feels redundant and unnecessary to relive the events, emotions, and chaos once you've lived through it—you may not survive it again. So in full disclosure, and in the spirit of the honesty of this beautiful book, this is my first venture back in time with Lesléa's poetry collection. It is remarkable how so much can be relayed in this form—all the emotions anyone experiences in these unholy situations are revealed. Not only the emotions but the facts, told in a way everyone can envision while reading every word.

A poet is a storyteller, and I believe the world is enlightened by the storyteller. History has been told and retold through the ages by the storyteller. We experience things differently through the words of the storyteller. We feel things through the words of the storyteller that may be new to us. These words may frighten us, make us laugh or cry, or cause us to feel anger, sadness, or loneliness. These words may even make us wonder about the purpose of our very existence. In short, these words force us to think and to question. My hope is that you, the reader, will experience all of this as you read through Lesléa's beautiful words and wonder: Why did this happen? Why does anything like this ever happen? And what can I do to make sure nothing like this ever happens again?

—*Judy Shepard*

Contents

Part Two

Introduction

On Tuesday, October 6, 1998, at approximately 11:45 p.m., twenty-one-year-old Matthew Shepard, a gay college student attending the University of Wyoming, was kidnapped from a bar by twenty-one-year old Aaron McKinney and twenty-one-year-old Russell Henderson. Pretending to be gay, the two men lured Matthew Shepard into their truck, drove him to the outskirts of Laramie, robbed him, beat him with a pistol, tied him to a buck-rail fence, and left him to die. The next day, at about 6:00 p.m. — eighteen hours after the attack — he was discovered and taken to a hospital. He never regained consciousness and died five days later, on Monday, October 12, with his family by his side.

One of the last things Matthew Shepard did that Tuesday night was attend a meeting of the University of Wyoming's Lesbian, Gay, Bisexual, and Transgendered Association. The group was putting final touches on plans for Gay Awareness Week, scheduled to begin the following Sunday, October 11, coinciding with National Coming Out Day. Planned campus activities included a film showing, an open poetry reading, and a keynote speaker.

That keynote speaker was me.

I never forgot what happened in Laramie, and around the tenth anniversary of Matthew Shepard's death, I found myself thinking more and more about him. And so I began writing a series of poems, striving to create a work of art that explores the events surrounding Matthew Shepard's murder in order to gain a better understanding of their impact on myself and the world.

What really happened at the fence that night? Only three people know the answer to that question. Two of them are imprisoned, convicted murderers whose stories often contradict each other (for example, in separate interviews both McKinney and Henderson have claimed that he alone tied Matthew Shepard to the fence). The other person who knows what really happened that night is dead. We will never know his side of the story.

This book is my side of the story.

While the poems in this book are inspired by actual events, they do not in any way represent the statements, thoughts, feelings, opinions, or attitudes of any actual person. The statements, thoughts, feelings, opinions, and attitudes conveyed belong to me. All monologues contained within the poems are figments of my imagination; no actual person spoke any of the words contained within the body of any poem. Those words are mine and mine alone. When the words of an actual person are used as a short epigraph for a poem, the source of that quote is cited at the back of the book in a section entitled "Notes," which contains citations and suggestions for further reading about the crime. The poems, which are meant to be read in sequential order as one whole work, are a work of poetic invention and imagination: a historical novel in verse. The poems are not an objective reporting of Matthew Shepard's murder and its aftermath; rather they are my own personal interpretation of them.

There is a bench on the campus of the University of Wyoming dedicated to Matthew Shepard, inscribed with the words *He continues to make a difference.* My hope is that readers of *October Mourning: A Song for Matthew Shepard* will be inspired to make a difference and honor his legacy by erasing hate and replacing it with compassion, understanding, and love.

Prologue

THE FENCE
(before)

Out and alone
on the endless empty prairie

the moon bathes me
the stars bless me

the sun warms me
the wind soothes me

still still still
I wonder

will I always be out here
exposed and alone?

will I ever know why
I was put on this earth?

will somebody someday
stumble upon me?

will anyone remember me
after I'm gone?

Part One

OUTNUMBERED

October 6, 1998
approximately 11:45 p.m.

There were about
6 billion people
in the world
that night

There were around
281 million people
in the United States
that night

There were perhaps
483 thousand people
in Wyoming
that night

There were maybe
26 thousand people
in Laramie
that night

There were roughly
20 people
in the Fireside Lounge
that night

There were precisely
3 people
in that Ford pickup
that night

2 triumphant
1 terrified

RECIPE FOR DISASTER

Take two local boys
(with hearts removed)
Place in bar
Add one pitcher of beer
Bring slowly to a boil

Toss in one gay college kid
(sweet and on the small side)
Add more alcohol
Stir together
Remove from bar

Add equal amounts
rage
hatred
ignorance
fear

Place heated mix in cab of truck
Wait for things to go sour

It won't take long

SOMETHING SNAPPED

Matt Shepard needed killin'.
— Aaron McKinney

I can't explain it.
He made me feel
jumpy. My blood
tore up my veins
like a black pickup
gunning down
the highway.
My heart pounded
like a fist
banging on a door
I didn't dare open.
I got hot
under the collar.
I was sweating
bullets.
Who did he think he was?
Just some queer dude
sitting pretty at the bar
swinging his sissy legs
sipping his prissy drink.
When I came
up behind him
he turned his head
something snapped
and I knew
I needed to take him out
for a ride
and show that little faggot
one hell of a time.

RAISING AWARENESS

Guess what? We're not gay.
You're going to get jacked.
  —Aaron McKinney

They were aware	He was unaware
he was alone	they were together
They were aware	He was unaware
he was frail	they were hard
They were aware	He was unaware
he was trusting	they were scheming
They were aware	He was unaware
he was gay	they were lying
They were aware	He was unaware
he was out	they were out
for fun	for blood
It was gay	He was caught
awareness week	unaware

EVERY MOTHER'S PLEA

I love you, too. Be safe.
—Judy Shepard
to her son Matthew

Buckle your seat belt.
Look both ways before you cross.
Don't talk to strangers.

THE TRUCK

I confess:

I was wildly driven

I took a wrong turn

I didn't steer clear

I didn't switch gears

I didn't slow down

I ignored the signs

I overheated

I blew a fuse

It wasn't an accident

ROAD RAGE

I am straight
and narrow

I am long
and lean

I am dusty
and dirty

I am cracked
and pocked

I've been stomped on
and tromped on

I've been stamped on
and tramped on

I've been driven on
and ridden on

I've been spit on
and shit on

I've been scorched by sun
and drenched by rain

I've been battered by wind
and pelted by snow

I've been run down
a million times

I've seen crashes
and pileups

I've seen roadkill
and carrion

I've seen blood
and guts and gore

I can take anything
I'm tough as time

But when I saw him
between the two of them

trapped in that truck
it made me want to heave

A SORRY STATE

Wyoming: Like No Place On Earth
—*Sign along the highway*

This is just to say
I'm sorry you came back to me:
the land of your birth
the land of your heart
the land that they call
the Equality State

Forgive me
for not teaching you
what every Cowboy knows:
once a player is out
he may not be safe
at home

SIGNS OF TROUBLE

Caution
Stop
Danger
Stop
Slow Down
Stop
Delay
Stop

Hazard
Stop
Turn Back
Stop
Keep Out
Stop
Wrong Way
Stop

Rough Road
Stop
Downhill
Stop
Blasting
Stop
Soft Shoulder
Stop

Yield
Stop
Dead End
Stop
Stop
Stop
Stop
Stop

THE CLOTHESLINE

He was bound with a real thin white rope.
— Officer Reggie Fluty

They strung me along
I got tangled up

They roped me in
I was fit to be tied

They yanked me around
I grew twisted and frayed

They straightened me out
I began to unravel

They bound me together
I got tied up in knots

They gave me a lashing
I was whipped into shape

They tore me to shreds
I held on by a thread

They stranded me
I was hung out to dry

THE PISTOL

It was a fearsome fifteen-inch long, three-pound weapon.
—*Bill Kurtis, narrator,* American Justice:
Matthew Shepard: Death in the High Desert

cold
hard
tough

solid
steeled
robust

hammered
loaded
triggered

half-cocked
ballistic
deadly

WITNESS

watching in horror
wishing he could do something:
the man in the moon

THE FENCE
(that night)

I held him all night long
He was heavy as a broken heart
Tears fell from his unblinking eyes
He was dead weight yet he kept breathing

He was heavy as a broken heart
His own heart wouldn't stop beating
He was dead weight yet he kept breathing
His face streaked with moonlight and blood

His own heart wouldn't stop beating
The cold wind wouldn't stop blowing
His face streaked with moonlight and blood
I tightened my grip and held on

The cold wind wouldn't stop blowing
We were out on the prairie alone
I tightened my grip and held on
I saw what was done to this child

We were out on the prairie alone
Their truck was the last thing he saw
I saw what was done to this child
I cradled him just like a mother

Their truck was the last thing he saw
Tears fell from his unblinking eyes
I cradled him just like a mother
I held him all night long

WHAT YOU CAN DO IN EIGHTEEN HOURS

Write a term paper
Cram for a final

Fly across the ocean
Drive cross-country

Scale a mountain
Run a marathon

Deliver a baby
Read *War and Peace*

Fall in love
Fall out of love

See the moon disappear
Watch the sun rise and set

Wait to be discovered
lashed to a fence

Shivering under a blanket
of stars

STARS

across

scattered

the

sky

in

blinking

dismay

unable

being

to help

light

years

away

THE WIND

The North Wind
carried his father's laugh
The South Wind
carried his mother's song
The East Wind
carried his brother's cheer
The West Wind
carried his lover's moan
The Winds of the World
wove together a prayer
to carry that hurt boy home

THE DOE

I heard
screeching brakes
slamming doors
scuffling feet
desperate pleas
chilling laughter
cracking bones
jagged groans
silence

I smelled
fury
terror
sorrow
blood

I tasted
fear
hesitation
and hunger
deep inside my gut
and crept softly
toward a tuft
of sagebrush

I saw
a beaten up
broken down
bent over
bruised
battered
busted
boy

I felt
the two fawns
in my belly
curl into a ball
as I snuggled
beside him
and struggled
to keep him
warm

WHERE IS MY BOY?

I knew how much he loved his cat.
— *Tina LaBrie, friend of Matthew Shepard*

Where is the soft boy who sits in the chair
with me on his lap and his hands in my hair?

Where is the sad boy who tickles my ears
while telling me all of his dreams and his fears?

Where is the sweet boy who loves me so much,
his whole face lights up at my purr or my touch?

Where is the boy? He's been out half the night.
This just isn't like him. It doesn't seem right.

Is he gazing at stars? Is he under the moon?
Is he sick? Is he hurt? Is he coming home soon?

Where is the boy? Will he ever be back?
I'm cold and I'm lonely and I need a snack.

Why has he left me alone for so long?
Where is my boy? I'm afraid. Something's wrong.

THE BIKER

I thought it was a joke.
—Aaron Kreifels,
mountain biker

It was near
Halloween

Folks were getting
spooky

Witches flew
across frozen front yards

Ghosts hung down
from cottonwood trees

Skeletons dangled
off rotten porch railings

I thought it was
a scarecrow's head

slumped over
that forsaken fence

not a smashed shattered
pumpkin of a boy

THE PATROL OFFICER'S REPORT

The only place that he didn't have any blood on him, on his
face, was what appeared to be where he'd been crying.
— Officer Reggie Fluty

two thin white tear tracks
one red swollen blood-caked face
this is someone's child

THE DOCTOR

The Doctor
keeps himself cold and hard
like the shiny silver stethoscope
slung around his neck

The Doctor
keeps his expression blank
like the crisp clean lab coat
covering his back

The Doctor
keeps his emotions in line
like the color-coded file folders
stacked neatly on his desk

The Doctor
keeps a stiff upper lip
like the unmoving mouths
of his patients in the morgue

The Doctor
keeps bawling
like a newborn
every time he sees

what's left of that boy

THE HOUSEKEEPER, ICU

I see them come
I see them go

I see them come
bruised burnt battered
bleeding busted up broken down

I see them come
I see them go

I see them go
dancing walking hobbling
on crutches in wheelchairs in body bags

I see them come
I see them go

I've been here more years
than that boy
been breathing

I see them come
I see them go

Work here long enough
you know
in your bones

I saw him come
I'll see him go

I know
he hasn't got a chance
in Hell

God wants him
going straight
to Heaven

LAME EXCUSE

Since our last medical update . . . Matthew Shepard
has remained in critical condition.
—*Rulon Stacey,*
CEO, Poudre Valley Hospital,
October 10, 1998

This is just to say
I'm sorry
I won't be in class tomorrow
or the day after that
or the day after that

Forgive me
I haven't a leg
to stand on
and I've learned
my lessons
too late

HOW TO HAVE THE WORST DAY OF YOUR LIFE

Hear something ringing in your sleep.
Open your eyes.
Reach for the clock.
See it is two or three or five in the morning.
Realize your alarm clock isn't ringing.
Realize your phone is ringing.
Feel dread fill your stomach like a rush of water.
Consider for a moment not answering the phone.
Know that not answering won't stop it from happening.
Know that whatever it is, it isn't good. Good news never comes
    at two or three or five in the morning.
Fumble for the phone.
Say hello.
Hear an unfamiliar voice say your name like a question.
Say, *It is I,* or *Speaking,* or *That's me,* or *Yes?*
Hear the unfamiliar voice say there's bad news.
Hear the unfamiliar voice say, "Are you sitting down?"
Sit up.
Know deep in your gut that after you hear this bad news, your life will
    never be the same.
Take a deep breath. Take another.
Feel nausea crawl its way up your throat.
Hear the unfamiliar voice say the word *accident.*
Hear the unfamiliar voice say the word *incident.*
Try to listen to the unfamiliar voice through the roaring in your ears.
Try to understand that someone you love very very much is very very
    hurt.
Try to believe this.
Try to deny this.
Try to understand this.
Try to accept this.
Take down the address and phone number you are given.
Hang up.
Throw up.
Throw some things into a bag.

Fly/drive/ride/run/walk/crawl to the hospital where
    your loved one lies bandaged, sedated, and hooked
    to machines.
Cry.
Sob.
Wail.
Pray.
Speak softly into your loved one's undamaged ear.
Say everything you need to say.
Take hold of your loved one's swollen hand.
Squeeze it gently.
Let go.

THE JOURNALIST

Fresh out of school
first day on the job
my editor sighed and said
here's all you need to know:
a real reporter would kill
his own grandmother
for a good story

Now, beat it

I beat it
I became a real reporter
for many years I came up
with many good stories
without killing my grandmother
or anyone else
or even thinking about it

until I came to Laramie

and saw a spiffed-up suited-up
made-up miked-up newscaster
shove aside a dozen people
to stick her nose
and camera
into his family's face
I could have killed her

It would have made a good story

VIGIL: CANDLES IN THE WIND

When the teacher
who praised him
lit me
I glowed

    When the friend
    who loved him
    lit me
    I flickered

        When the lover
        who knew him
        lit me
        I trembled

            When the stranger
            who grieved him
            lit me
            I quivered

                Across the country
                around the world
                one by one
                by one

                    We appeared
                    to light up
                    the night
                    like stars

                        Until one by one
                        by one like stars
                        we faded
                        into mourning

THE ARMBANDS

*We have made and distributed over 3,000 yellow armbands
with green circles in our community alone.*
— *Jesus Rios, student president,
University of Wyoming*

Though we are worn
we are not weary

Though we are flimsy
we are not weak

Though we are yellow
we are not afraid

Though we are green
we are not naive

Though we are tattered
we are not broken

Though we are torn
we are not divided

Though we are fading
we are not giving up

Though we are many
we are standing as one

SCARED TO DEATH

After they hustled me into their truck
After they hustled me out of their truck
After they called me those horrible names
After they laughed and spit in my face
After they beat me and beat me and beat me
After they bound my hands to the fence
After they roared away in their truck
After they finally left me alone
After a night that lasted forever
After the sun rose and shone in my eyes
After a biker stumbled upon me
After an ambulance took me away
After my body was hooked to machines
After my family sobbed at my side
After my photo was shown on the news
After the vigils were held in my name
An angel appeared with her wings open wide
And I wasn't afraid anymore

HEARTFELT APOLOGY

This is just to say
I'm sorry
I kept beating
and beating
inside
your shattered chest

Forgive me
for keeping you
alive
so long
I knew it would kill me
to let you go

OCTOBER 12, 1998

Poudre Valley Hospital
Fort Collins, Colorado

Somebody entered the world with a cry
Somebody left without saying good bye

NOW SHOWING: *MATTHEW'S STORY*
(film titles of 1998)

How to Make the Cruelest Month
A Simple Plan
Meeting People Is Easy
Dangerous Beauty
Gods and Monsters
Dark City
Safe Men

Ride
The Hi-Lo Country
No Looking Back
Out of Sight
The Siege
The Imposters
Psycho
Slam
The Big Hit
Disturbing Behavior
Killing Time
Very Bad Things

Riddler's Moon
Eternity and a Day
Permanent Midnight
Twilight
Savior
The Last Days
Desperate Measures
In God's Hands
Hope Floats
God Said, Ha!
Hush
Last Night
Dead Man on Campus

The Object of My Affection
Beloved
Ever After
Celebrity
Holy Man
Urban Legend
Deep Impact
Since You've Been Gone
Wide Awake
Trance
Who Am I?
What Dreams May Come

TREE

I knew the time was coming
for me to become something
glorious and I was not afraid

When I heard the buzz
of the lumberjack's saw
I welcomed that first cut

for I'd dreamed of this moment
for hundreds of years
and the possibilities were endless

a wall where a beautiful painting hangs
a table where a beautiful dinner steams
a chair where a beautiful woman sits

a floor for a dancer to leap upon
a page for a poet to scrawl upon
a pad for an artist to draw upon

a letter sent to a stationed soldier
a letter sent to a secret lover
a letter sent to Santa Claus

a top that spins at breakneck speed
a yo-yo swinging from a string
a carved horse on a carousel

a serving spoon a salad bowl
a rolltop desk a rocking chair
a jewelry box a picture frame

but never in my wildest dreams
a small oak chest filled to the brim
with ashes that once were a boy

CLASS PHOTO: ME IN THE MIDDLE
OR
"WHAT WILL YOU BE WHEN YOU GROW UP?"

Astronaut!
Ballerina!
Clown!
Dancer!
Elephant Trainer!
Firefighter!
Gymnast!
Hip-Hop Artist!
Ice Skater!
Juggler!
Karate Master!
Lifeguard!
martyr
Newspaper Reporter!
Opera Star!
Pirate!
Queen of the Universe!
Rap Singer!
Spy!
Tightrope Walker!
UPS Driver!
Veterinarian!
Waiter!
X-Men Comic Book Hero!
Yo-yo Champ!
Zookeeper!

THEN AND NOW

Then I was a son
Now I am a symbol

Then I was a brother
Now I am an absence

Then I was a friend
Now I am a memory

Then I was a person
Now I am a headline

Then I was a guy
Now I am a ghost

Then I was a student
Now I am a lesson

THIRTEEN WAYS OF LOOKING AT MATTHEW

I
Son

II
Brother

III
Friend

IV
Lover

V
Faggot

VI
Target

VII
Victim

VIII
Casualty

IX
Tragedy

X
Martyr

XI
Hero

XII
Legend

XIII
Star

Part Two

THE FENCE
(one week later)

I have seen people come out here with a pocketknife
and take a piece of the fence, like a relic, like an icon.
— *Rev. Stephen M. Johnson, Unitarian minister*

I keep still
I stand firm
I hold my ground
while they lay down

flowers and photos
prayers and poems
crystals and candles
sticks and stones

they come in herds
they stand and stare
they sit and sigh
they crouch and cry

some of them touch me
in unexpected ways
without asking permission
and then move on

but I don't mind
being a shrine
is better than being
the scene of the crime

STAND BY YOUR MAN

I was protecting someone I loved.
— *Chastity Pasley, twenty-one-year-old girlfriend*
of Russell Henderson

He came home with guilt in his eyes
He came home with blood on his hands
He came home with nothing to lose
He came home with something to hide

He told me he'd been to a bar
He told me he'd been with a friend
He told me he beat someone up
He told me he needed a plan

We threw ourselves into the car
We threw his clothes into the trash
We threw his shoes into a shed
We threw our story together

Now I have guilt in my eyes
Now I have blood on my hands
Now I have nothing to lose
Now I have something to hide

ACCESSORY

I asked him, "What's wrong?" and he said, "I think I killed someone."
—Kristen Price, eighteen-year-old girlfriend
of Aaron McKinney

A cat-shaped pin with rhinestone eyes
Barrettes that look like butterflies

A necklace strung with purple shells
An anklet hung with silver bells

A beaded purse made out of suede
A leather hair tie for my braid

A tiny turquoise pinkie ring
A heart of gold upon a string

A sorry, cheap accessory—
that's what some folks are calling me

I wish that night had never come
Oh, how could I have been so dumb?

OFFICER OF THE COURT

Some days this courtroom feels so cold
it chills me to the bone

Look at those boys
shivering in their suits
> *They left him out in the cold to die*

Like to knock both
their heads together
> *They bashed in his skull with the butt of a gun*

The one on the left
is shaking in his boots
> *They even stole his goddamn shoes*

The one on the right
looks about to cry
> *They beat him harder when he wept for his life*

Look at those boys
staring down at their hands
> *They bound his hands to a buck-rail fence*

Listen to those boys
pleading for mercy
> *They left him lying in a pool of blood*

Some days this courtroom feels so cold
it chills me to the bone

HIS SHOES

small
lightweight
sporty
stylish

handsome
sexy
soft
striking

upscale
well heeled
classy
polished

cared for
elegant
sophisticated
smooth

dashing
daring
dapper
delicate

pointed to
laughed at
spit on
snatched

tied up
scratched up
messed up
beat up

worn out
broken
discarded
ruined

irreplaceable

THE FRAT BOYS

Colorado State University
Fort Collins, Colorado
October 10, 1998

Hey, wouldn't it be funny
Hey, wouldn't it be hysterical
Hey, wouldn't it be a riot

to make our scarecrow
the scarecrow on our float
the scarecrow on our homecoming float

look like a homo
look like a queer
look like a freakin' fairy?

Hey, that would be funny
Hey, that would be hysterical
Hey, that would be a riot

Like that fag from Wyoming
that fag they tied to the fence
that fag they thought was a scarecrow

Let's write I LIKE BOYS on his shirt
Let's write I'M GAY on his hat
Let's write I LOVE DICK on his pants

Hey, that's really funny
Hey, that's really hysterical
Hey, that's really a riot

Hey, that'll knock 'em dead

THE SONGWRITER

I scritch scratch scrawl
my pen across the page

I hum strum thrum
my fingers across the guitar

I stand step stare
out the window

hoping to find
the one perfect word

that escapes me
like a bird soaring out of sight

a ship sailing out to sea
a dream dissolving into air

I know
that one perfect word

is waiting to be caught
like a ball in a mitt

a fish in a net
a heart in a throat

I know
that one perfect word

is out there
and will catch me

off guard
arriving

in perfect time
like it always does

making my song
perfect

but not perfect
enough

to bring him to life

THE DRAG QUEEN

If I were a homosexual in Laramie,
I would hang low, very low.
        — Carla Brown, manager
        Fireside Lounge

The minute it happened
my silver sequin slingbacks
slid back
into the closet

The minute it happened
my glittery gold gowns
slipped back
into the closet

The minute it happened
my fluffy feather boas
slithered back
into the closet

The minute it happened
my wavy waist-length wigs
slumped back
into the closet

The minute it happened
I dragged my sorry ass
back
into the closet

slapped the door shut

and swallowed the key

THE COP

I was a rotten son of a bitch when it came
to dealing with gay issues.
  — *Dave O'Malley, police commander*

the day I heard
the words
fag
faggot
fairy
sissy
pussy
lezzie
lesbo
homo
dyke
bulldyke
diesel
pervert
he/she
freak
fruit
pansy
queen
and queer
flew out
of my mouth
for good

THE BARTENDER

I still replay and think about it.
—*Matt Galloway, bartender, Fireside Lounge*

If only I had known
my face would be
the last friendly face
he'd ever see
If only I had known

If only I had known
my voice would be
the last friendly voice
he'd ever hear
If only I had known

If only I had known
my hand would be
the last friendly hand
he'd ever high-five
If only I had known

If only I had known
I'd have said
Dude, wait up
I'll take you home
I've got a truck
If only I had known

If only I had known

LET'S SAY

Let's say
you felt
kind of restless
that night

Let's say
you felt
kind of horny
that night

Let's say
you went
to the bar
that night

Let's say
you drank
a few beers
that night

Let's say
you glanced
his way
that night

Let's say
you thought
he was hot
that night

Let's say
your heart
skipped a beat
that night

Let's say
you almost
walked over
that night

Let's say
you felt
too shy
that night

Let's say
you felt
too scared
that night

Let's say
you feared
being teased
that night

Let's say
you feared
being hurt
that night

Let's say
you finished
your drink
that night

Let's say
you went
home alone
that night

Let's say
you beat
yourself off
that night

Let's say
you had
sweet dreams
that night

Let's say
you can't
forget
that night

How will
you live
the rest
of your life?

THE STUDENT

When I heard what happened
I stopped
breathing

When I heard what happened
I started
crying

When I heard what happened
I stopped
eating

When I heard what happened
I started
shaking

When I heard what happened
I stopped
sleeping

When I heard what happened
I started
retching

When I heard what happened
I stopped
cruising

When I heard what happened
I started
praying

When I heard what happened
I told
my family

When I heard what happened
I told
my friends

When I heard what happened
I told
the world

I'm gay and it could have been me

A FATHER

Hell, I got a kid that age.
Back east. In college.
Don't know what he does all day.
Goes to classes, I hope.
For my money, he better be
studying, not fooling around.
He's not the brightest bulb
on the tree. Too trusting.
Always has been.
Never uses his head.
A real follower.
Soft. A mama's boy.
Used to come home crying.
Never learned to use his fists.
I told him a thousand times
not to talk to strangers.
People will do anything.
You can't be too careful.
Especially nowadays.
Tell you what.
If I ever catch my kid
getting into a car
with two lousy punks
he met at some cowboy bar,
I'll take my belt
to him, grown as he is.
I'll break every bone
in his goddamn body.
I'll kick his ass
clear to the moon
and back. I'll—
What? What did they say?
That kid in Wyoming
died? He up and died?
God damn it.
Jesus H. Christ.

A MOTHER

Hate is not a Laramie value.
—posted on signboard
in front of University Inn,
Laramie, Wyoming

I sit at my table
pick up my pen
and write to the folks
of that poor murdered boy

I tell them I live
in the heart of this town
and feel all torn up
when I think of their son

I tell them I hate
what happened and say
if I can do anything
give me a call

I tell them I go
to mass every Sunday
but I don't agree
with what the priest says

I tell them my son
lives up at the college
and means more to me
than both of my hands

I tell them straight out
who cares if he's gay
as long as he's happy
it's all right by me

Then I put down my pen
tear my letter in half
and lay my head down
on my cold folded arms

A CHORUS OF PARENTS

Go home, give your kids a hug, and don't let a day go by
without telling them you love them.
—Judy Shepard, October 12, 1998

I called my son
I called my oldest my youngest my middle my only my—say it—
    gay son
I called my son
I called my sixteen-year-old, eighteen-year-old, twenty-five-year-old,
    thirty-seven-year-old, fifty-six-year-old son
I called my son
I called my son who hasn't heard my voice in a week a month a year
    two years five years a decade forever
I called my son
I called my son who came out when he was fourteen, fifteen, nineteen,
    twenty-two, thirty-two, fifty-two, a week ago, a month ago,
    a year ago, five years ago, half a century ago
I called my son
I called my son who lives in New York, San Francisco, L.A., Paris,
    Provincetown, Boston, Montreal, Tennessee
I called my son
I called my son who never stopped sending me Christmas, Chanukah,
New Year's, Mother's Day, Father's Day, Passover, birthday cards
I called my son
I called my son whom I'd chewed out kicked out threw out threw up
    on hung up on turned my back on sat shivah for lied about
    denied deserted abandoned
I called my son
I called my son to say I'm sorry forgive me I've changed I was wrong
    I love you, I need you, I miss you, come home
I called my son
I called my son
He wasn't there
I pray he calls me back

THE CHURCH LADY

God looked down
and said
nothing

God looked down
and did
nothing

I looked up
to God
once upon a time

Now he does
nothing
for me

A PROTESTOR

God Hates Fags, Matt in Hell
—Signs held by anti-gay protestors at Matthew
Shepard's funeral and the trials of his murderers

The only good fag is a fag that's dead
He asked for it, you got that right
The fires of Hell burn hot and red

A boy who takes a boy to bed?
Where I come from that's not polite
The only good fag is a fag that's dead

A man and a woman, the Good Lord said
As sure as Eve took that first bite
The fires of Hell burn hot and red

I hear upon his knees he pled
Fairies don't know how to fight
The only good fag is a fag that's dead

Beneath the Hunter's Moon he bled
That must have been a pretty sight
The fires of Hell burn hot and red

C'mon, kids, it's time for bed
Say your prayers, kiss Dad good night
The only good fag is a fag that's dead
The fires of Hell burn hot and red

AN ANGEL

Before you stands a band of angels.
— Romaine Patterson, founder of Angel Action, whose members
dressed as angels with seven-foot wings to block out anti-gay
protestors at the trials of Matthew Shepard's murderers

Angels need not fear to tread
Look evil squarely in the face
Lift your wings above your head

and block the folks who like to spread
their hate and lies from place to place
Angels need not fear to tread

Love thy neighbor, as it's said
Short of that, give them their space
Lift your wings above your head

Stitch by stitch and thread by thread
Weave wings of gossamer and lace
Angels need not fear to tread

Dressed in white as if to wed
Stand tall with dignity and grace
Lift your wings above your head

Say your prayers, God bless the dead
Being gay is no disgrace
Angels need not fear to tread
Lift your wings above your head

JURY SELECTION

Prosecutors to Seek Death Penalty in Beating
—New York Times *December 29, 1998*

No
No I
No I would
No I would not
No I would not hesitate
No I would not hesitate to kill
No I would not hesitate to kill the killer
No I would not hesitate to kill the killer in a heart beat   in a heart beat
No I would not hesitate to kill the killer
No I would not hesitate to kill
No I would not hesitate
No I would not
No I would
No I
No

THE PROSECUTOR'S JOB

You have a person that is tied to a fence, five-foot-two,
105 pounds, begging for his life. . . . He [McKinney] could
have stopped [beating Shepard] but he chose not to.
— *Cal Rerucha, prosecuting attorney*

his job
his only job
his one and only job

is to prove that no doubt
without a shadow of a doubt
beyond any reasonable doubt

the defendant
the savage
the monster

deliberately
purposefully
intentionally

committed
carried out
executed

a robbery
a kidnapping
a killing

which cannot be excused
which cannot be forgiven
which cannot be undone

the rest is irrelevant
the rest is history
the rest is baloney

he rests his case

THE DEFENSE'S JOB

What happened here is beyond comprehension. It's disgusting.
It's tragic. But it's not premeditated murder. . . . Is it that bad
that this person has to be erased from the planet?
                    —*Dion Custis, defense attorney*

his job
his only job
his one and only job

is to protect
is to preserve
is to spare

the client's
the criminal's
the killer's

life

even if no one else thinks
even when no one else thinks
even though no one else thinks

the brute's
the bastard's
the son of a bitch's

life

is barely worth
is hardly worth
is just not worth

saving
redeeming
a damn

DON'T FLATTER YOURSELF

The thought of a gay guy approaching him and
humiliating him . . . I guess it just set him off.
—Kristen Price, girlfriend of Aaron McKinney

It's a come-on
you think
if he looks
your way

It's a come-on
you think
if he smiles
your way

It's a come-on
you think
if he waves
at you

It's a come-on
you think
if he speaks
to you

It's a come-on
you think
if he stands
with you

It's a come-on
you think
if he sits
with you

It's a come-on
you think
if he goes
to your school

It's a come-on
you think
if he goes
to your church

It's a come-on
you think
if he lives
on your street

It's a come-on
you think
if he lives
in your world

Oh, come on

Don't you think he's got
better things to do
than risk his life
to come on to you?

SORRY BOY

Judge Rejects "Gay Panic"
as Defense in Murder Case
—New York Times *November 2, 1999*

This is just to say
I'm sorry
to deny
your request
to use
the gay panic defense

Forgive me
for pointing out
the obvious:
there was someone gay
and panicked that night
but that someone wasn't you

LOGIC PROBLEM

*I would say it wasn't a hate crime. All I wanted
to do was beat him up and rob him.*
                                    — *Aaron McKinney*

5'2"
105 pounds
21 years old

Hit in the head 18 times
with 4 fists
and a .357 Magnum

18 hours lashed
to a 2-rail buck fence
in 30-degree weather

All for 20 bucks
and 1 pair of black
patent-leather size 7 shoes?

It doesn't add up

VERDICT

YOU, Mr. McKinney, are:

Guilty of Kidnapping:
Using lies to trick and fool him like
"**I** like you" and "I'm gay," **YOU**
Lured him to your pickup
Truck and drove him miles away.
YOU, Mr. McKinney, are

Guilty of Robbery:
Unloading twenty bucks
Into the pocket of your pants, **YOU**
Left him broke and
Terrified without a backward glance.
YOU, Mr. McKinney, are:

Guilty of Murder:
Unleashing rage and hatred with
Intent to maim and hurt, **YOU**
Laughed to see him suffer as he
Tasted blood and dirt.
YOU, Mr. McKinney, are:

GUILTY
GUILTY
GUILTY

MERCY

At the bitter end,
a matter of life and death:
Mercy. For the boy.

WHAT TWENTY BUCKS COULD GET YOU IN 1998

19 dozen eggs
or 7 pounds of bacon

21 loaves of bread
or 5 pounds of coffee

6 gallons of milk
or 47 pounds of sugar

20 heads of lettuce
or 12 gallons of gas

5 Big Macs served with fries
or 2 life sentences served back to back

WOUNDED

You know, my mom was killed in Laramie.
She was raped, and then the guy just left her
on the side of the road.

— *Russell Henderson*

the kid
who beat
that mama's boy
and left
him to die
wounded
like an animal
strung up
on a fence
in the middle
of nowhere
with nothing
to comfort him
but the howl
of the cold
Wyoming wind

heard his own mama

had been beaten
and raped
by someone
else's son
who left
her to die
wounded
like an animal
on the side
of the road
with nothing
to comfort her
but a thin
white blanket
of wet Wyoming snow

THIS IS THE HAND

I'm still trying to figure it out;
why I did what I did.
— Russell Henderson

This is the hand
that slapped him
silly

This is the hand
that hit him
hard

This is the hand
that smacked him
senseless

This is the hand
that beat him
blind

This huge hairy hand
with its sharp
pointed knuckles

This big beefy hand
scarred and stained
with his blood

This is the hand
that taunts me
each morning

This is the hand
that haunts me
each night

This is the hand
that won't leave
my mind

This is the hand
that won't leave
my arm

ONCE UPON A TIME

I don't like gay people. As far as Matt is concerned,
I don't have any remorse.

—*Aaron McKinney*

Once I hung out in bars
Now I hang out behind bars

Once I had a housemate
Now I have a cellmate

Once I had a life
Now I have a life sentence

Once my son looked up to me
Now the world looks down on me

Once I felt pent up and angry
Now I am pent up and angry

Once I hated faggots
Now I hate them more

THE FENCE
(after)

The fence has been torn down.
— *New York Times*

prayed upon
frowned upon

revered
feared

adored
abhorred

despised
idolized

splintered
scarred

weathered
worn

broken down
broken up

ripped apart
ripped away

gone
but not forgotten

Epilogue

PILGRIMAGE

The land was sold and a new fence now stands
about fifty yards away. People still come to pay
their respects.
　　—*Jim Osborn, friend of Matthew Shepard*

I walk to the fence with beauty before me
The Lord is my shepherd; I shall not want

I walk to the fence with beauty behind
me
Yit'gadal v'yit'kadash

I walk to the fence with beauty above me
Om Mani Padme Hum

I walk to the fence with beauty below me
Blessed are the meek, for they shall inherit

I reach the fence surrounded by beauty
wail of wind, cry of hawk

I leave the fence surrounded by beauty
sigh of sagebrush, hush of stone

Afterword

IMAGINE

For Matthew Shepard
December 1, 1976–October 12, 1998

Before Monday, October 12, 1998, I could never have imagined myself sobbing onstage in front of hundreds of people. Nor could I ever
have imagined being greeted by a college administrator who had tears
streaming from his eyes. But that is exactly what happened on the day
I arrived at the University of Wyoming, the school Matthew Shepard
had attended before he died from one of the most brutal gay bashings
of all time. Ironically, it was the start of Gay Awareness Week, and
I was the event's keynote speaker. Since the talk I had been invited
to give, *"Heather Has Two Mommies:* Homophobia, Censorship, and
Family Values," focuses on how education can end prejudice and
hatred, my appearance in Laramie couldn't have been more timely.

A few days before my trip to Wyoming, Jim Osborn, the chair of
the school's Lesbian, Gay, Bisexual, and Transgendered Association,
called to tell me what had happened to Matthew. "I thought you should
know," he said, "and I wouldn't blame you if you decided not to come."

I only had one question: had the perpetrators been caught?

"They're already in jail," Jim assured me.

"Then I'll be there," I assured him. Given the circumstances, I knew
how important it was for the University of Wyoming students to go on
with Gay Awareness Week. And I was not going to disappoint them.

The student who picked me up at Denver International Airport
was polite, quiet, and obviously saddened and shaken by what had just
happened in her town. As we drove through an endless afternoon—I
learned that in Wyoming a "short ride from the airport" means a good
three hours—my eyes wandered the landscape. To this native New
Yorker, the vast empty spaces were terrifying. It was easy to see how a
young man who had been beaten unconscious and left to die lashed to
a fence could remain undiscovered for eighteen hours.

As we pulled into Laramie, I spotted television trucks with satel-
lite dishes parked outside the pawnshops and bars. My driver proudly
pointed out the tallest building in Wyoming: a student dormitory that

boasted eight floors. "What's your state population?" I asked my new friend.

"About four hundred fifty thousand," she answered, and then her eyes filled. "Minus one."

When we finally arrived on campus, I was met by the bodyguard I'd requested, who took me right to my lecture hall. Jim Osborn greeted me warmly and tied a yellow ribbon for Matthew around my sleeve before we fell weeping into each other's arms.

Why was I feeling so emotional? Why did I care so much about Matthew Shepard? I had never met him or even heard his name until a few days before my arrival. I subscribe to many gay newspapers, and unfortunately I read about gay bashings all the time. And while I always get terribly upset to read about such horrific events, being at Matthew's school, meeting his friends and teachers, and knowing that he had planned on attending my lecture, filled me with an unspeakable sadness. And a touch of fear.

Matthew's attackers were in jail only a stone's throw away, at least by Wyoming's standards. Russell A. Henderson and Aaron J. McKinney were to be arraigned the next day, and despite my trepidation, I wished I didn't have an early-morning flight, so I could show up in court. Like Yoko Ono, who pressed her nose to the glass of the police cruiser that held Mark David Chapman the night he shot John Lennon, I, too, wanted to look at the faces of those who could be that cruel.

I started my presentation by asking for a moment of silence for Matthew Shepard. Then I addressed the LGBT students in the audience, who I knew were feeling particularly vulnerable and needed special words of encouragement to go on despite their rage, sorrow, and fear. Next I addressed the heterosexual members of the audience, reminding them that they had a unique opportunity to show the world what kind of allies they were. Finally, I asked every member of the audience to think of one thing they could do to help put a stop to homophobia and to promise the person next to them that they would do that one thing before the week was through. Then I launched into my speech.

After my presentation, I sat behind a book table and talked with dozens of students. Each one of them shook my hand, thanked me for coming, and told me how much my visit meant to them. I realized that the students in Wyoming didn't need to hear my speech as much as they needed to see me, an out, proud lesbian, right before their very eyes. I knew what my presence communicated to them: if my life was possible, their lives and the lives of their friends were possible, too.

The morning after my talk, I found myself at the airport in a tram heading for Terminal C. A woman who looked about my age smiled and pointed to my yellow armband. "What's that?"

"It's for Matthew Shepard," I explained.

Her eyes filled with tears. "His poor parents," she said. "I can't imagine what they're going through."

As the tram raced along, the phrase *I can't imagine* repeated itself over and over in my mind. So many people I'd spoken to in the last twenty-four hours had said the same thing: *I can't imagine.* And yet we must imagine, because the truth is, what happened to Matthew Shepard and his family could happen to any one of us. My guess is that the woman I'd met at the airport was a mother. Perhaps she had a son. Perhaps she had a gay son, and she couldn't imagine herself watching her child die from wounds so violently, viciously, and deliberately inflicted.

I have tried my hardest to imagine the last hours of Matthew Shepard's life before he lost consciousness. It is impossible to fathom the raw fear he surely felt as he begged for his life. As a poet, I know it's part of my job to use my imagination. It's part of my job as a human being, too. Because only if each of us imagines that what happened to Matthew Shepard could happen to any one of us will we be motivated to do something. And something must be done.

The morning that Matthew Shepard died, Jim Osborn, along with two gay organizations in Colorado, received e-mail messages saying, "Congratulations on the faggot being beaten to death there in Wyoming! I hope it happens more often!" Even as Matthew lay dying in Fort Collins, a homecoming parade for Colorado State University passed his hospital bed a few blocks away. A fraternity float in the parade featured a scarecrow with the words *I'm Gay* painted on it, referring to the fact that the first person who happened upon Matthew thought he was a scarecrow and almost didn't stop. Members of the Westboro Baptist Church had the gall to picket Matthew Shepard's funeral with signs that said, *God Hates Fags* and *Matt in Hell.* The Internet is full of gay-hating organizations, and while I believe passionately in freedom of speech, I believe more passionately in freedom and justice for all.

And to that end, I hope that each reader of *October Mourning: A Song for Matthew Shepard* will think of one thing to do to help end homophobia and do it this week. Write a pro-gay letter to a state representative or your local newspaper. Donate money to the Matthew

Shepard Foundation. Start a gay-straight alliance at your high school. Join the LGBT student group at your college or university. Put a "safe zone" sticker on your office door. Integrate a lesson about gay history into your classroom curriculum. Buy a set of freedom rings and wear them around your neck. March in your local gay pride parade. Hang a rainbow flag outside your door. Call a gay or lesbian friend just to say "I love you."

I left Laramie on October 13, 1998, with a small photo of Matthew Shepard, which I tucked into my wallet. To this day, I take it out and look at it every time I get on a plane and fly to a new city to give a speech about gay rights. Looking at Matthew Shepard's picture reminds me why I do the work I do: so that what happened to him will never happen again. I gaze at the face of the young man I never had the chance to meet, and whisper a traditional Jewish prayer for peace that includes the words: *and you shall lay down and no man shall terrify you.*

To quote John Lennon: Imagine.

Explanation of Poetic Forms

p. 7: "Every Mother's Plea" is a haiku. A haiku is a Japanese form of poetry that consists of three lines. The first line contains five syllables, the second line contains seven syllables, and the third line contains five syllables. The last line of the poem often contains a moment of sudden awareness or epiphany.

p. 11: "A Sorry State" is modeled after the poem "This Is Just to Say" by William Carlos Williams.

p. 12: "Signs of Trouble" is a found poem, meaning that it consists of text found in everyday life (in this case road signs) that was not originally meant to be a poem.

p. 15: "Witness" is a haiku. See "Every Mother's Plea" for an explanation of the form.

p. 16: "The Fence (that night)" is a pantoum. A pantoum is a Malayan form of poetry consisting of four-line stanzas. The second and fourth lines of each stanza become the first and third lines of the next stanza. And then the first and third lines of the first stanza are repeated in the last stanza, so that every line of the poem is used twice.

p. 18: "Stars" is a concrete poem. In a concrete poem, the appearance of the poem — how it physically takes up space on the page — adds to its meaning. In this poem, the words are scattered across the page to represent stars scattered across the sky.

p. 22: "Where Is My Boy?" is written in rhymed couplets.

p. 24: "The Patrol Officer's Report" is a haiku. See "Every Mother's Plea" for an explanation of the form.

p. 27: "Lame Excuse" is modeled after the poem "This Is Just to Say" by William Carlos Williams.

p. 33: "Scared to Death" is a list poem. A list poem is just what it sounds like: a list or catalog of items or events. It often uses repetition.

p. 34: "Heartfelt Apology" is modeled after the poem "This Is Just to Say" by William Carlos Williams.

p. 36: "Now Showing: *Matthew's Story*" is a found poem. See "Signs of Trouble" for an explanation of the form. In this poem, the found text consists of titles of movies released in 1998.

p. 39: "Class Photo: Me in the Middle" is an alphabet poem. The letters *A* to *Z* are used as the first letters of the twenty six words of the poem in alphabetical order.

p. 41: "Thirteen Ways of Looking at Matthew" is modeled after the poem "Thirteen Ways of Looking at a Blackbird" by Wallace Stevens.

p. 47: "Accessory" is written in rhymed couplets.

p. 66: "A Protestor" is a villanelle. A villanelle consists of six stanzas: the first five stanzas contain three lines, and the final stanza contains four lines. The first line and the third line of the first stanza serve as the last line of the next four stanzas. In the final stanza, these lines appear as the third and fourth line (the last two lines of the poem). A villanelle also contains a rhyme scheme of *aba* in the first five stanzas, and *abaa* in the final stanza.

p. 67: "An Angel" is a villanelle. See "A Protestor" for an explanation of the form.

p. 68: "Jury Selection" is a concrete poem. See "Stars" for an explanation of the form. In this poem, the words on the page are meant to resemble a syringe holding a lethal injection.

p. 73: "Sorry Boy" is modeled after the poem "This Is Just to Say" by William Carlos Williams.

p. 75: "Verdict" is an acrostic. In an acrostic, when read downward, the first letters of the words of the poem form a word. In this case, the word *guilty* is spelled out three times going down the page.

p. 76: "Mercy" is a haiku. See "Every Mother's Plea" for an explanation of the form.

p. 85: "Pilgrimage": The first line of each stanza of this poem is modeled after a traditional Navajo prayer. The second lines of the first four stanzas are taken from prayers from other traditions as follows:

The second line of the first stanza is taken from the twenty-third Psalm.

The second line of the second stanza is taken from the Kaddish, the Jewish mourner's prayer.

The second line of the third stanza is taken from the traditional Tibetan Buddhist prayer of compassion.

The second line of the fourth stanza is taken from Matthew 5:5.

Discussion Questions

1. In her introduction to *October Mourning,* Lesléa Newman explains that "the poems are not an objective reporting of Matthew Shepard's murder and its aftermath"; they are the author's "own personal interpretation" (page xvii). Her notes at the end of the book reveal how deeply she drew from the reporting of others. How do facts and imagination intertwine throughout this book?

2. A truck, a road, a deer, and even a length of rope (pages 8, 9, 20, and 13, respectively) offer their perspectives on the deadly October night. Why do you think the author decided to give voices to these normally silent witnesses?

3. How does an ordinary person become a martyr? In "Class Photo: Me in the Middle" (page 39), Matthew's classmates are described as future ballerinas or karate masters, but he's labeled a martyr. Children aspire to greatness in ballet or karate; does any child want to grow up to be a martyr? How is the memory of a martyr kept alive?

4. While Matthew Shepard was dying at a nearby hospital, some fraternity brothers in Fort Collins, Colorado, mocked his suffering at their university's homecoming parade (page 51). Why would they behave that way? Why is cruelty sometimes disguised as humor?

5. "Mercy. For the boy" (page 76). Matthew Shepard's father spoke out against the death penalty for his son's killers. Why do you think Mr. Shepard took this stance?

6. How does the form of a poem shape its meaning and its impact? How, for example, would a concrete poem like "Stars" (page 18) be different if it were written as a haiku, like "Every Mother's Plea" (page 7)?

7. In the prologue of this book, the fence wonders "will anyone remember me/after I'm gone?" (page xxi). How does the poem "The Fence (after)" (page 82) answer that question?

8. Matthew Shepard was the victim of a hate crime, which is defined by the FBI as a "criminal offense against a person or property motivated in whole or in part by an offender's bias against a race, religion, disability, sexual orientation, ethnicity, gender, or gender identity." Learn what you can about hate crimes that have been committed in your own community. Who was targeted? How were the criminals punished, if at all? Are steps being taken to prevent more hate crimes in your community?

9. More than twenty years have passed since Matthew Shepard was killed. Do you think a similar atrocity could happen now? To whom? Why?

Notes

p. 3: "Outnumbered": According to *The Meaning of Matthew: My Son's Murder in Laramie, and a World Transformed,* by Judy Shepard, "McKinney, Henderson, and Matt left the Fireside Lounge at about 11:45 at the earliest" (p. 149). The statistics in stanzas 1–4 are from the U.S. Census Bureau website, http://www.census.gov/.

p. 5: "Something Snapped": Epigraph: Quote taken from an interview conducted by Greg Pierotti in *The Laramie Project—Ten Years Later: An Epilogue,* by Moisés Kaufman and the Members of the Tectonic Theater Project (p. 44). On page 42 of the same script, the text of which is taken from interviews, McKinney states, "The night I did it, I did have hatred for homosexuals" (the word *it* referring to Matthew Shepard's murder). Nate Green, in a *Laramie Boomerang* article titled "McKinney's Taped Confession," published on October 29, 1999, reported that in his taped confession, McKinney referred to Matthew Shepard as "some queer dude." And in an interview published on page 38 of *The Advocate* on January 28, 2000, David McNeill, a prisoner at Wyoming State Penitentiary, described Aaron McKinney as "marching around the jail exclaiming, 'Do you know who I am? I'm the one that killed that fag.'"

p. 6: "Raising Awareness": Epigraph: Sergeant Rob Debree, lead investigator for the Albany County Sheriff's Department, quotes Aaron McKinney as saying these words in the *New York Times* article "Witnesses Trace Brutal Killing of Gay Student," by James Brooke, published on November 21, 1998. The article also quotes Sergeant Debree as saying, "Before savagely beating Matthew Shepard with a pistol butt, one of his tormentors taunted him, saying, 'It's Gay Awareness Week.'"

p. 7: "Every Mother's Plea": Epigraph: Quote attributed to Judy Shepard taken from "The Crucifixion of Matthew Shepard," by Melanie Thernstrom, published in *Vanity Fair,* March 1999.

p. 11: "A Sorry State": This epigraph is one of Wyoming's state slogans and can be seen on bumper stickers and road signs throughout the state. A photo of a road sign bearing this slogan can be seen on Flickr: http://www.flickr.com/photos/justanotherhuman/869945960/. Wyoming is nicknamed both the Equality State and the Cowboy State. Athletic teams at the University of Wyoming are named the Cowboys.

p. 12: "Signs of Trouble": According to the *New York Times* article "Witnesses

Trace Brutal Killing of Gay Student," by James Brooke, published on November 21, 1998, "An autopsy found that Mr. Shepard had been hit 18 times in the head. He was also bruised on the backs of his hands, indicating that he had tried to protect himself." The word *stop* appears in this poem eighteen times to represent those eighteen blows.

p. 13: "The Clothesline": Epigraph: Officer Reggie Fluty's quote is taken from *The Laramie Project* by Moisés Kaufman and the Members of the Tectonic Theater Project (p. 37).

p. 14: "The Pistol": Epigraph: Spoken by Bill Kurtis, narrator of the HBO documentary *American Justice: Matthew Shepard: Death in the High Desert.* According to the *New York Times* article "Gay Man Beaten and Left for Dead; 2 Charged," by James Brooke, published on October 10, 1998, McKinney and Henderson "tied their captive to a fence and pistol-whipped him with a .357 Magnum handgun 'while he begged for his life.'"

p. 15: "Witness": According to the U.S. Naval Observatory website, the night of the assault, the moon was one day past full. http://aa.usno.navy.mil/cgi-bin/aa_moonphases.pl?year=1998&ZZZ=END.

p. 17: "What You Can Do in Eighteen Hours": According to the *New York Times* article "After Beating of Gay Man, Town Looks at Its Attitudes," by James Brooke, published on October 12, 1998, Laramie police were asserting that Aaron McKinney and Russell Henderson kidnapped Matthew Shepard and "left him tied to a ranch fence for 18 hours until a passing bicyclist spotted Mr. Shepard, who was unconscious."

p. 20: "The Doe": According to Judy Shepard's memoir, *The Meaning of Matthew: My Son's Murder in Laramie, and a World Transformed,* when Officer Reggie Fluty arrived at the fence, a large doe was lying near Matthew Shepard, "as if the deer had been keeping him company through the night" (p. 162).

p. 22: "Where Is My Boy?" Epigraph: Tina LaBrie's quote appears in "The Crucifixion of Matthew Shepard," by Melanie Thernstrom, published in *Vanity Fair,* March 1999. According to the same article, after Matthew Shepard died, Tina LaBrie adopted his cat, Clayton.

p. 23: "The Biker": Epigraph: Quote taken from "Still Searching: Shepard Changed Lives," by Kerry Drake, *Casper Star-Tribune,* October 7, 2008, http://www.trib.com/news/state-and-regional/article38bab2c6-c5fe-5c6f-9889-33e1485ea981.html: "Eighteen hours later, Kreifels was riding his mountain bike by a buck-and-rail fence west of the city when he spotted what looked like a scarecrow tied near the bottom of it. 'At first I thought it was a joke,' Kreifels said . . . Upon closer examination, he realized it was a human being whose face was covered with blood. Kreifels rode to the nearest house to get help, and police arrived."

p. 24: "The Patrol Officer's Report": Epigraph: According to Patrol Officer Reggie Fluty's testimony at Aaron McKinney's trial, "The only place that he didn't have any blood on him, on his face, was what appeared to be where he'd been crying down his face." Court TV excerpt of Officer Fluty's testimony appears in a Matthew Shepard Foundation Organizational video, http://vimeo/6150007.

p. 25: "The Doctor": According to a medical report issued by Poudre Valley Hospital in Fort Collins, Colorado, Matthew Shepard was admitted on Wednesday, October 7, 1998, in critical condition. According to a hospital statement given at 3:00 p.m. on October 10, "Matthew's major injuries upon arrival consisted of hypothermia and a fracture from behind his head to just in front of the right ear. This has caused bleeding in the brain, as well as pressure on the brain. There were also approximately a dozen small lacerations around his head, face and neck" (Matthew Shepard Online Resources Archive, http://www.wiredstrategies.com/shepard4.html).

p. 27: "Lame Excuse": Epigraph: Poudre Valley Hospital released medical updates about Matthew Shepard's condition from the time he was admitted on October 7, 1998, until the time of his death, five days later. This quote is from the hospital statement given on October 10, 1998, at 9:00 p.m. (Matthew Shepard Online Resources Archive, http://www.wiredstrategies.com/shepard4.html).

p. 31: "Vigil: Candles in the Wind": As Matthew Shepard lay in a coma, candlelight vigils were held for him all over the world. According to *Losing Matt Shepard: Life and Politics in the Aftermath of Anti-Gay Murder*, by Beth Loffreda, "As the weekend continued, vigils for Matt were held across the nation. By the end of the week, we'd heard word of vigils in Casper, Cheyenne, and Lander (Wyoming towns), Colorado, Idaho, Montana, Iowa, Arizona, Rhode Island, and Pennsylvania" (p. 13).

p. 32: "The Armbands": Epigraph: Quote taken from a statement released by Jesus Rios, student president of the University of Wyoming, on October 12, 1998: "Friends and fellow students of the University of Wyoming, ask for your support in remembering Matthew Shepard. We have made and distributed over 3,000 yellow armbands with green circles in our community alone, and encourage every community to do the same. It is to remember the tragedy which has occurred on our campus, and to encourage the political fight which Matthew himself was a part of. We ask that all institutions of higher education seek out all institutional policies to include equality on the basis of sexual orientation, and that they take an active role in educating students, faculty and staff" (Matthew Shepard Online Resources archive, http://www.wired strategies.com/shepard4.html).

p. 35: "October 12, 1998": Matthew Shepard died on October 12, 1998, at 12:53 a.m., with his family by his side. ("University of Wyoming Posts Statements to Web," University of Wyoming Spectrum website, http://uwacad web.uwyo.edu/spectrum/mattnews.htm).

p. 36: "Now Showing: *Matthew's Story*": This poem consists of titles of films released in 1998 (Nash Information Services website, http://www.the-numbers.com/movies/index1998.php).

p. 38: "Tree": According to *The Meaning of Matthew: My Son's Murder in Laramie, and a World Transformed,* by Judy Shepard, Matthew Shepard was cremated and his ashes put into a "small oak chest with a ceramic mountain scene on top" (p. 138).

p. 45: "The Fence (one week later)": Epigraph: Quote taken from the *New York Times* article "Wyoming City Braces for Gay Murder Trial," by James Brooke, published on April 4, 1999. According to "The Crucifixion of Matthew Shepard," by Melanie Thernstrom, published in *Vanity Fair,* March 1999, the fence where Matthew Shepard was tied became "a place of pilgrimage. Barren and beautiful beneath the snow-dusted Rockies, the site conjures thoughts of Golgotha. Small yellow stones have been arranged to form a cross; in every crevice of the fence are bouquets, notes, stray tokens."

p. 46: "Stand By Your Man": Epigraph: Quote taken from "Girlfriend of Shepard's Convicted Murderer Testifies," CNN.com, October 28, 1999, http://cgi.cnn.com/US/9910/28/shepard.trial.01/. According to the same article, "Chastity Pasley, 21, is serving an 18-month prison sentence after pleading guilty to being an accessory after the fact in the slaying of Matthew Shepard. . . . She said she had misgivings about getting involved and was 'mad at myself' the next day as she, Henderson and McKinney's girlfriend, Kristen Price, drove to Cheyenne to dump Henderson's clothes in a gas station Dumpster. . . . She said they hid expensive shoes Henderson had been wearing that night in a shed in Cheyenne owned by her mother."

p. 47: "Accessory": Epigraph: Quote taken from the *Newsweek* article "The 'Gay Panic' Defense," by Joshua Hammer, published on November 8, 1999 (p. 40). According to the *Tampa Tribune*'s November 10, 1999, "Nation/World in Brief," Kristen Price was initially charged as an accessory after the fact in connection with Matthew Shepard's murder. She pled guilty to the lesser charge of interfering with a police officer and was sentenced to 180 days in jail, receiving 120 days' credit for time served, with the remaining 60 days suspended. According to *Merriam-Webster's Collegiate Dictionary*, an accessory is someone who contributes to the commission of a crime or who afterward helps the person who committed the offense with the intent of eluding justice.

p. 48: "Officer of the Court": According to the *New York Times* article "Gay Man Beaten and Left for Dead; 2 Are Charged," by James Brooke, published on October 10, 1998, "At the Albany County courthouse here, Russell A. Henderson, 21, and Aaron J. McKinney, 22, were arraigned on charges of kidnapping, aggravated robbery and attempted first-degree murder." According to *Merriam-Webster's Collegiate Dictionary*, the term "officer of the court" refers to court personnel, including judges, bailiffs, and clerks, as well as lawyers in their dealings with courts and the judicial system.

p. 49: "His Shoes": According to the *New York Times* article "Gay Man Beaten and Left for Dead; 2 Are Charged," by James Brooke, published on October 10, 1998, Laramie Police Commander Dave O'Malley said that "After nearly beating the young man to death, the assailants stole his wallet and shoes and left him tied to the fence."

p. 51: "The Frat Boys": According to "The Crucifixion of Matthew Shepard," by Melanie Thernstrom, published in *Vanity Fair*, March 1999, "On Saturday afternoon, a few blocks from the hospital bed where Matthew's parents were keeping vigil, a Colorado State University homecoming parade passed by. On a *Wizard of Oz* float sponsored by the Pi Kappa Alpha fraternity and Alpha Chi

Omega sorority, the scarecrow character had been defaced. Scrawled in black spray paint was I'M GAY, as well as anti-homosexual obscenities."

p. 52: "The Songwriter": Many songs have been written for and about Matthew Shepard, including "Scarecrow," by Melissa Etheridge, "Matthew," by Janis Ian; and "American Triangle," by Elton John.

p. 54: "The Drag Queen": Epigraph: Quote taken from the *New York Times* article "Gay Man Beaten and Left for Dead; 2 Are Charged," by James Brooke, published on October 10, 1998.

p. 55: "The Cop": Epigraph: Quote taken from Commander Dave O'Malley's interview in the HBO documentary *American Justice: Matthew Shepard: Death in the High Desert*. After Matthew Shepard was murdered, Commander O'Malley, deeply affected by Matthew Shepard's death, became a gay-rights activist, sometimes speaking at events alongside Judy Shepard.

p. 56: "The Bartender": Epigraph: Quote taken from the *Casper Star Tribune* article "Still Searching: Shepard Changed Lives," by Kerry Drake, published on October 7, 2008, http://www.trib.com/news/state-and-regional/article_38bab2c6-c5fe-5c6f-9889-33e1485ea981.html. According to the same article, "Galloway was the last person to talk to Shepard . . . before he was fatally beaten by two men on the outskirts of Laramie shortly after midnight on October 7, 1998. . . . He said he was overwhelmed by guilt because he didn't stop his young friend from leaving the bar with his killers. 'You just replay it a thousand times in your head, but you just never know what's going to happen,' he said. 'I've come to terms with it, but I will never fully—I still replay it and think about it.'"

p. 63: "A Mother": Epigraph: Quote taken from a motel sign filmed in Laramie, Wyoming, and shown in *The Laramie Project*, HBO Home Video.

p. 64: "A Chorus of Parents": Epigraph: Quote taken from a Shepard family statement read by Rulon Stacey, CEO, Poudre Valley Hospital, 4:30 a.m., October 12, 1998, the day Matthew Shepard died. The entire statement can be found in *The Meaning of Matthew: My Son's Murder in Laramie, and a World Transformed*, by Judy Shepard (pp. 133–134).

p. 66: "A Protestor": Epigraph: Signage from photographs taken outside the

Albany County Courthouse in Laramie, Wyoming, by Dan Cepeda and published in the *Casper Star-Tribune* on April 6, 1999 (p. A-1) and October 12, 1999 (p. A-1). A photograph taken by Dan Cepeda of a similar sign that was held outside Matthew Shepard's funeral by an anti-gay protestor can be seen at the *Casper Star-Tribune* website, http://trib.com/uploaded-photos/image_e52422f0-8801-5569-b679-b7dc160bd910.html.

p. 67: "An Angel": Epigraph: Quote taken from a press release by Romaine Patterson released in Laramie, Wyoming, on April 5, 1999. The full text of the press release can be found on Romaine Patterson's website, http://www.eatromaine.com/1/laramie-angels.html. Romaine Patterson is one of the founders of Angel Action, a group that combats homophobia by dressing as angels and standing silently in front of anti-gay protestors to block out their messages of hate. The press release states, "Our focus is to bring forth a message of peace and love." Further information about Angel Action can be found in Romaine Patterson's memoir, *The Whole World Was Watching: Living in the Light of Matthew Shepard*.

p. 68: "Jury Selection": Epigraph: Headline of a *New York Times* news brief published on December 29, 1998. Because prosecutor Cal Rerucha intended to seek the death penalty for Aaron McKinney and Russell Henderson, jurors had to be willing to put these two men to death for their crimes. Russell Henderson avoided a trial by changing his plea to guilty. He received two back-to-back life sentences. In a *New York Times* article, "Gay Murder Trial Ends with Guilty Plea," published on April 6, 1999, James Brooke reported, "Escaping a possible death penalty, Russell A. Henderson was sentenced by District Judge Jeffrey A. Donnell for his part in the beating, robbery, and murder of the student, Matthew Shepard, here six months ago."

p. 69: "The Prosecutor's Job": Aaron McKinney was prosecuted by County Attorney Cal Rerucha. The first part of the epigraph is taken from the HBO documentary *American Justice: Matthew Shepard: Death in the High Desert*. The second part is taken from an article titled "Defense Argues Manslaughter in Closing Statements," by Heather Gierhart, in the University of Wyoming newspaper, *The Branding Iron*, November 3, 1999.

p. 70: "The Defense's Job": Aaron McKinney was defended by defense attorneys Dion Custis and Jason Tangeman. Epigraph: The first part of the epigraph is taken from the *New York Times* article "Man Is Convicted of Killing Gay Student" by Michael Janofsky, published on November 4, 1999. The second part is taken from the HBO documentary *American Justice: Matthew Shepard: Death in the High Desert*.

p. 71: "Don't Flatter Yourself": Epigraph: Quote taken from an interview broadcast on ABC *World News Tonight* on Sunday, October 11, 1998, 11:10 p m EDT, as reported in "ABC Interviews Girlfriend and Father of Assailant," University of Wyoming Specgrum website, http://uwacadweb. uwyo.edu/spectrum/mattnews.htm. Aaron McKinney's attorneys tried to use a "gay panic" defense, alleging that McKinney became so panicked from a perceived gay advance that he was not responsible for his actions. According to *The Meaning of Matthew: My Son's Murder in Laramie, and a World Transformed*, by Judy Shepard (p. 227), McKinney's defense lawyer Jason Tangeman said, "The evidence is going to show that it is the advance of Mr. Shepard—the homosexual advance of Mr. Shepard—that was significant to Aaron McKinney. . . . That humiliated him in front of his friend Russell Henderson. His past just bubbled up in him. . . . And in his own words, he left his body."

p. 73: "Sorry Boy": Epigraph: Headline of a *New York Times* article by Michael Janofsky published on November 2, 1999. The article goes on to say, "A District Court judge in Laramie, Wyo., ruled today that lawyers for a man accused of murdering a gay college student last year may not use a 'gay panic' defense to justify the actions of their client. . . . The judge, Barton R. Voigt, told the lawyers that their effort to demonstrate a panic defense was little more than an attempt to show that their client, Aaron J. McKinney, had suffered temporary insanity or diminished capacity when he admittedly killed the student, Matthew Shepard, by beating him with a pistol in a fit of rage. Neither defense is recognized by Wyoming law."

p. 74: "Logic Problem": Epigraph: Quote taken from an interview with Aaron McKinney conducted by Elizabeth Vargas on *20/20*, November 26, 2004 ("New Details Emerge in Matthew Shepard's Murder," ABC News website: http://abcnews.go.com/2020/story?id=277685&page=1.TzvJgRyBVX8.

p. 75: "Verdict": According to the *New York Times* article "Man Is Convicted in Killing of Gay Student," by Michael Janofsky, published on November 4, 1999, "A jury in Laramie Wyo., today found a man [Aaron McKinney] guilty of second-degree murder in the killing of a gay University of Wyoming student last year. By also finding him guilty of robbery and kidnapping, the jury enabled prosecutors to seek a death penalty."

p. 76: "Mercy": Epigraph: Quote taken from Dennis Shepard's statement to the court, given on November 4, 1999, which concludes with these words: "I would like nothing better than to see you die, Mr. McKinney. However, this is the time to begin the healing process. To show mercy to someone who refused to show any mercy. Mr. McKinney, I am going to grant you life, as hard as it is for me to do so, because of Matthew. . . . May you have a long life, and may you thank Matthew every day for it." The full text of Dennis Shepard's statement can be found in *The Meaning of Matthew: My Son's Murder in Laramie, and a World Transformed*, by Judy Shepard (pp. 234–247). A video of Dennis Shepard reading his statement can be found on YouTube, http://www.youtube.com/watch?v=xkQysLewF4w.

p. 77: "What Twenty Bucks Could Get You in 1998": Prices from *The Value of a Dollar, 1860–2004*, third edition, Millerton, NY: Grey House Publishing, 2004, and *Oil and Gas Journal*, October 1998. Aaron McKinney was given two back-to-back life sentences with no chance of parole. According to the *New York Times* article "Parents of Gay Obtain Mercy for His Killer," by Michael Janofsky, published on November 5, 1999, "Responding to a request from the court-appointed lawyers for Mr. McKinney, prosecutors consulted with the Shepard family and agreed to accept two consecutive life sentences rather than to push for the death penalty. In exchange, Mr. McKinney relinquished his right to appeal."

p. 78: "Wounded": Epigraph: Quote taken from an interview conducted by Steve Belber in *The Laramie Project—Ten Years Later: An Epilogue* by Moisés Kaufman and the Members of the Tectonic Theater Project (p. 31). According to a *Casper Star-Tribune* article, "Man Pleads Guilty in Death of Henderson's Mother" published on July 24, 1999, (p. B-1) the body of Russell Henderson's mother, forty-year-old Cindy Dixon, "was discovered on a snow-covered rural road about eight miles north of Laramie" on January 3, 1999. According to the same article, twenty-eight-year-old Dennis Leroy Menefee Jr. "was accused of picking up Dixon on a street corner, sexually abusing her and then kicking her out of his vehicle on a bitter winter night." Menelee pled guilty to manslaughter.

p. 79: "This Is the Hand": Epigraph: Quote taken from an interview conducted by Steve Belber in *The Laramie Project—Ten Years Later: An Epilogue*, by Moisés Kaufman and the Members of the Tectonic Theater Project (p. 31).

p. 81: "Once Upon a Time": Epigraph: Quote taken from an interview conducted by Greg Pierotti in *The Laramie Project—Ten Years Later: An Epilogue*, by Moisés Kaufman and the Members of the Tectonic Theater Project (p. 44).

p. 82: "The Fence (after)": Epigraph: Quote taken from the *New York Times* article "Laramie Killing Given an Epilogue a Decade Later," by Patrick Healy, published on September 17, 2008.

p. 85: "Pilgrimage": Epigraph: Quote taken from an author interview with Jim Osborn in Laramie, Wyoming, April 2010. As Jim told me, several years after Matthew Shepard's murder, the land where the tragedy occurred was sold. A long buck fence now stands on the property about fifty yards east of where the original three-section, split-rail fence once stood. People still visit the site to leave offerings such as notes and flowers, say prayers, and pay their respects. On April 11, 2010, I visited the site and said Kaddish for Matthew Shepard. As I chanted the traditional Jewish mourner's prayer, two hawks flew overhead.

Resources

BOOKS

Kaufman, Moisés, and the Members of the Tectonic Theater Project. *The Laramie Project.* New York: Vintage Books, 2001.

Loffreda, Beth. *Losing Matt Shepard: Life and Politics in the Aftermath of Anti-Gay Murder.* New York: Columbia University Press, 2000.

Patterson, Romaine. *The Whole World Was Watching: Living in the Light of Matthew Shepard.* New York: Alyson Books, 2005.

Shepard, Judy. *The Meaning of Matthew: My Son's Murder in Laramie, and a World Transformed.* New York: Hudson Street Press, 2009.

SCRIPT

Kaufman, Moisés, and the Members of the Tectonic Theater Project. *The Laramie Project—Ten Years Later: An Epilogue.* On October 12, 2009, the eleventh anniversary of Matthew Shepard's death, this play was performed simultaneously in all fifty states and several countries. An audience guide to the production can be found at https://www.tectonictheaterproject.org/wp-content/uploads/2018/07/Audience_Guide_to_Laramie_Epilogue.pdf.

NEWSPAPERS AND MAGAZINES

More than seventy *New York Times* articles about Matthew Shepard's murder and its aftermath can be found at the *New York Times* website under *Times Topics,* http://topics.nytimes.com/topics/reference/timestopics/people/s/matthew_shepard/index.html?s=oldest&

The full text of "The Crucifixion of Matthew Shepard," by Melanie Thernstrom, published in *Vanity Fair* in March 1999, is posted at https://www.vanityfair.com/news/1999/13/matthew-shepard-199903.

DVDs

American Justice: Matthew Shepard: Death in the High Desert. A&E Television Networks, 2001.

The Laramie Project. HBO Home video, 2002.

Seckinger, Beverly. *Laramie Inside Out: An Inspiring Story of Personal Discovery and the Meaning of Community.* 2004. Information at http://laramieinsideout.com/index.shtml.

ARCHIVES

Matthew Shepard Collection, 1983–2008
University of Wyoming American Heritage Center
1000 E. University Avenue
Laramie, WY 82071
http://ahc.uwyo.edu

This collection contains public and private documents regarding Matthew Shepard's murder and its aftermath, including articles from the *Branding Iron* (University of Wyoming's student newspaper), the *Laramie Boomerang*, and the *Casper Star-Tribune,* as well as letters and e-mails from private collections that were donated to the archive.

WEBSITES

The Matthew Shepard Foundation
http://www.matthewshepard.org

Matthew's Place
https://medium.com/matthews-place

The Trevor Project
866-4U Trevor
(866-488-7386)
www.thetrevorproject.org
The Trevor Project provides crisis intervention and suicide prevention to LGBTQ youth.

Human Rights Campaign
http://www.hrc.org

PFLAG (Parents, Families, and Friends of Lesbians and Gays)
http://pflag.org

The author at the fence in Laramie, Wyoming, April 11, 2010

LESLÉA NEWMAN is the author of more than seventy books for readers of all ages, including the children's classic *Heather Has Two Mommies*, the middle-grade novel *Hachiko Waits*, and the picture books *Sparkle Boy*, *Gittel's Journey: An Ellis Island Story*, and *Ketzel, the Cat Who Composed*. Her award-winning short story "A Letter to Harvey Milk" has been adapted for the stage.

She has been awarded poetry fellowships from the National Endowment for the Arts and the Massachusetts Artists Foundation as well as two American Library Association Stonewall Honors and the National Jewish Book Award. From 2008 to 2010, she served as the poet laureate of Northampton, Massachusetts.

In addition, she works closely with the Matthew Shepard Foundation as a member of their speakers' bureau. She has visited schools all over the country giving her presentation "He Continues to Make a Difference: The Story of Matthew Shepard." Lesléa Newman lives in Massachusetts.